The history of emigration from

ITALY

Katherine Prior

FRANKLIN WATTS
A Division of Grolier Publishing
NEW YORK • LONDON • HONG KONG • SYDNEY
DANBURY, CONNECTICUT

© Franklin Watts 1997

First American Edition 1998 by
Franklin Watts
A Division of Grolier Publishing Co., Inc.
Sherman Turnpike
Danbury, Connecticut 06813

A CIP catalog record for this book is available
from the Library of Congress.

ISBN 0-531-14450-X

Editor: Sarah Snashall
Series editor: Rachel Cooke
Designer: Simon Borrough
Picture research: Sue Mennell

Printed in Malaysia

Picture acknowledgements

t=top; b=bottom; m=middle
AKG, London pp. 7b, 12b, 13,
Andes Press Agency pp. 9b (Carlos Reyes), 12t (Hugo
Fernandez)
Archives of Ontario p.17b (F1405 series/sub: 021-068
MSR no. 11903#1)
Archives of the United Church of Canada, Victoria
University, Toronto, Ontario p.16b (No. 90.115P675)
Corbis-Bettmann/UPI pp. 3, 15t and b, 19b, 21t
and b, 23b, 26t
Giancarlo Costa pp. 8b, 11t, 14, 19t, 20
Susan Cunningham p.13 insert
Eye Ubiquitous p.6t
Robert Harding pp. 5t, 6m
Holt Studios International p.25t (Nigel Cattlin)
Hulton Getty pp. 6b, 7t, 8t, 9t, 10t and b, 11b, 22t,
23t, 26b
Hutchison Library p.4
Image Bank pp. 16t, 25b, 27
Magnum Photos pp. 17t (T. Hoepker), 24 (David
Seymour)
Reproduced by courtesy of the trustees,
The National Gallery, London p.5b
Network p.29t (Barry Lewis)
Rex Features pp. 28, 29b
Ronald Grant Archive/Paramount Pictures p.18
Scottish Highland Photo Library p.22b

Contents

A Divided Country

By 1876, 100,000 Italians were leaving Italy every year.

Italy is the narrow, boot-shaped peninsula that juts out of southern Europe into the Mediterranean Sea. From its rocky shores Italians have travelled and settled all over the world.

Mass emigration from Italy began in the 1860s and lasted for about 100 years. By 1876, 100,000 Italians were leaving Italy every year. By 1900 this had risen to 500,000. Many Italians came and went two or three times before finally deciding whether to settle abroad or back home, but by 1940 there were at least 14 million Italians living outside Italy.

Many Countries within One

Italy is a mountainous country. The green, snowcapped Alps form Italy's northern border, and ridges of the dry, rocky Apennines run all the way down the peninsula to the toe of the "boot" and on to the island of Sicily. In the past, the mountains kept Italians from different areas separate from each other. People living in one valley had little contact with people in neighboring valleys. These different communities developed their own distinctive dialects and customs.

Until the mid-19th century, Italy was not a united country. Instead, the separate regions were each ruled by different kings or dukes. However, Italy was unified in 1861 by a group of devoted patriots who longed to see their country become one of the strong nations of Europe. In March 1861, Victor Emmanuel II was crowned king of all Italy.

As the map shows, Italy is a mountainous country. The mountains divide Italy into regions with separate identities. In the 19th century, when Italians thought of home, they did not think of Italy itself, but rather of their village and the countryside around it, their *paese*.

▶ A Catholic priest blesses a child outside St. Peter's Basilica in Rome. Religion still plays an important part in the lives of many Italians.

▼ A detail from *The Annunciation* by Fra Filippo Lippi, one of the great painters of the Italian Renaissance.

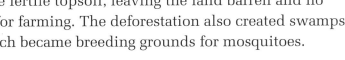

A Common Religion and Heritage

One thing Italians have always shared is the Roman Catholic religion. The Pope, the head of the worldwide Roman Catholic Church, lives in the Vatican State in Rome in central Italy. The Catholic Church has been led from Rome since the early years of Christianity.

Italians also share a glorious history. From the 14th to the 16th centuries, Italy produced wonderful advances in art, literature, science, philosophy, and architecture, based on the earlier achievements of classical Greece and Rome. This period is known as the Renaissance, which means "rebirth." During the Renaissance, artists and intellectuals all over Europe thought of the Italians as the most civilized and cultivated people in the world.

Overpopulation, Poverty, and Unemployment

By the time of unification in 1861, it seemed as if Italy's glory days were a thing of the past. Italy was now a poor country. It did not have sufficient raw materials like iron and coal to start up its own factories, and most people worked as peasants, shepherds, or agricultural laborers.

The population was expanding rapidly, from 18 million in 1800 to 26 million in 1860, to 40 million in 1930. This caused a shortage of farm land, but as people began cutting down trees to make room for more crops, rain washed away the fertile topsoil, leaving the land barren and no good for farming. The deforestation also created swamps, which became breeding grounds for mosquitoes.

▲ ▼ **The north of Italy (above) is wetter and more fertile than much of the land in the south, which is often dry and arid, such as the rocky island of Sicily (below).**

▼ **19th-century Italian farm laborers.**

Mosquitoes carry the disease malaria, and by the 1850s thousands of peasants had been weakened or killed by this and other types of disease.

North and South

These problems were particularly bad in southern Italy. The northern provinces had bigger cities and more industry and employment than the south. In northern Italy, too, the land and climate were better for farming, and if work was scarce, northerners could travel across the border to Austria and Switzerland to find work. In southern Italy, the dry, rocky landscape made farming unreliable, but it was still the main source of work. If the crops failed, there was little else to do.

By the 1860s, a large number of northern Italians began to think about finding work farther away than just across the border. They followed a smaller number of earlier emigrants, the travelling craftsmen and seasonal workers who had been leaving the country for centuries and who had established small Italian communities throughout Europe.

Art and Craft Abroad

There was already a long tradition of seasonal workers and skilled artists travelling worldwide, seeking their fortunes.

By the time mass emigration from Italy began in the 1860s, there was already a long tradition of seasonal workers and skilled artists travelling worldwide, seeking their fortunes.

Chimney Sweeps

From at least the 16th century, young boys from the Vigezzo Valley in Piedmont worked as chimney sweeps in France, Austria, Germany, and the Netherlands, cleaning the long brick chimneys of the multi-level buildings that existed in the bigger cities. It was dangerous and dirty work. The boys, aged from 10 to 15, were employed by a boss or patron (*padrone*) who took them to cities like Amsterdam and Paris to work, usually for about five years.

When they grew up, some of the sweeps became patrons (*padroni*) themselves, setting up their own chimney-sweeping businesses and bringing more boys from their home villages to the big, foreign cities.

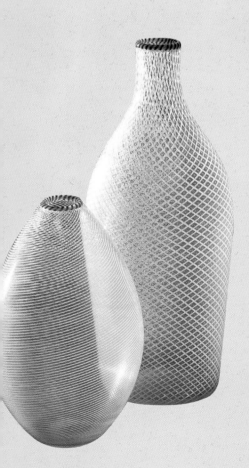

▼ Delicate glassware from Venice was treasured all over Europe and North America.

▶ A 19th-century chimney sweep. The life of a chimney sweep was dirty and dangerous.

Skilled Craft Workers Abroad

Other seasoned travellers were craft workers from northern Italy who carried skills perfected during the Renaissance all over Europe and sometimes even farther abroad: to North America, Asia, and Australia. Plaster workers from Lucca in Tuscany were famous for their handmade statues of saints and nativity figures. Mosaic makers travelled from Maniago in Friuli, creating pictures on floors, walls, and tabletops out of marble or small pieces of ceramic. The fragile glassware produced by the glassblowers of Venice was in demand in all the rich European cities; so too were the imaginative and elaborate confections of Italy's chocolate and ice-cream makers.

Settling Down Abroad

Most of the travelling workers had no intention of leaving Italy permanently and would return home every year or two with the savings they had made abroad. Often they had small farms back in Italy that their wives managed for them while they were abroad. By the 1860s and 70s, however, factories in Great Britain, Germany, and the United States had begun to churn out cheap, machine-made glass and plaster ornaments and metal items, which destroyed much of the craft workers' market. Their sales dwindled with the competition, and the craft workers found it harder and harder to survive.

For some, the answer was to surrender their land and emigrate to the bustling industrial cities, which they knew well from their travels, and try to make a permanent living there. As they were used to selling their goods in foreign streets, craft workers found other street work relatively easily, such as shoe shining and fruit selling. Some of the men took laboring jobs, as waterside workers or construction workers. Drawing on their business skills, others opened barber shops, restaurants, cafés, and grocery stores.

▲ An Italian shop in London in 1906. By 1900, corner shops selling Italian breads, olives, meats, and cheeses had sprung up in the "Little Italy" suburbs of all the major European and U.S. cities.

▼ Giovanni David, one of the leading Italian opera singers of the 19th century. Italian opera singers travelled throughout Europe and the Americas in the 19th century.

Musicians and Street Performers

Musicians were luckier than the craft workers; their skills did not go out of fashion with the rise of industrialization. By the 1850s, many Italian musicians and singers lived in London, Paris, Vienna, New York, and Buenos Aires. They gave music lessons to wealthy families and sometimes also performed publicly in the city streets.

Italian organ-grinders, pipers, and dancing-bear keepers also made a living on the streets of the big cities of

▲ A young Italian boy plays his harp on a London street in 1872.

▼ The Italian religious procession of the Madonna del Carmine in Clerkenwell, London. There has been an Italian community in Clerkenwell since the 1840s.

Europe and the Americas. In London by the 1840s, organ-grinders from northern Italy had established a small Italian suburb, or "Little Italy," around the streets of Hatton Garden and Leather Lane. They were poor men, and most had walked all the way from their home villages in Italy to London. As the Italian population grew, Italian organ manufacturers followed the musicians to London.

But it wasn't an easy life. Most street performers did not own their instruments but rented them from their *padroni,* who could take the instruments back if they didn't earn enough money. They were also often accused by local residents of spreading disease and of being pickpockets and beggars, and many cities passed bylaws to stop the Italians from working in the streets.

The Chain of Emigration Begins

By about 1860, small communities of Italians had been created in all the major cities of Europe and also in New York and Chicago in the United States and Buenos Aires in Argentina. Most were made up of people who came from the north of Italy and who had a history of travelling back and forth between their home and foreign countries.

Each time these travellers returned home with news of their success abroad, more Italians would be tempted to follow their old neighbor. Most did not want to leave permanently but dreamed of earning enough money to buy a good-sized farm back in their home village.

To South America

Immigrants who worked hard were warmly welcomed.

By the 1860s more Italians were beginning to venture farther abroad in their seasonal migrations. Some went all the way to Brazil and Argentina in South America for the coffee and grape harvests, returning home each year in time for the spring sowing in Italy.

Hardworking Immigrants Wanted Here!

In the mid-19th century, Brazil, Argentina, and other South American countries urgently required workers to develop their economies. The native Indian populations had been driven off their lands, and the governments now wanted to open up the land for coffee, sugar, wheat, and cattle production. Much of South America was rich in minerals like bauxite, silver, tin, and copper, and workers were needed for its mines and heavy industries. Immigrants who worked hard were warmly welcomed.

Three Million Newcomers

From 1875 until 1914, over three million Italians immigrated to South America. Until the 1890s most of these were from northern Italy. They included agricultural

▼ Italian women were left in Italy while the men were forced by poverty to seek work abroad.

▲ The silver mines of South America needed a large workforce. Italian emigrants were a vital extra labor source.

laborers, poor fishermen, and the sons of farmers whose land did not provide enough work for the whole family.

Usually adult men would go first, and only once they had established a steady income would they send for their wives and children to join them. An unmarried man might ask his parents to choose a wife for him from his village and send her out to him. Some men never sent for their families. They concentrated on saving up enough money to buy more land or pay off debts back in Italy, and they returned home once they had achieved this.

▲ Not all Italians prospered in Brazil. Some who worked on the coffee plantations were badly paid and poorly treated by the plantation managers.

In the Cities: Workers and Bosses

Italians formed big communities in the Brazilian city of São Paulo and in the Argentine city of Buenos Aires. By 1890, one in every three people living in Buenos Aires was an Italian. Italians made up over half of the city's factory workers, and richer Italians owned half of the city's factories. Numbering so many, the Italian workers were able to form strong trade unions and ensure that they earned good wages.

Moneymaking in Peru

Italian business success was especially remarkable in Peru. There were only about 15,000 to 20,000 Italians, mainly from Liguria, living there. Many had had some experience in Italy of small businesses, such as fishing ventures, and between 1890 and 1930 they developed much of Peru's oil, sugar, and textile industries. By 1930, Italians controlled over half of Peru's banks and much of its insurance industry and owned at least 100 factories.

▲ The main street of São Paulo, Brazil, in 1905, showing the Banco Italiano.

▲▼ The Italians brought their artistic influences to Argentina. In 1908 the Italian community in Buenos Aires opened the Colón Opera House (above), which established Buenos Aires as one of the world's leading cities for opera. The tango (below) is a blend of Spanish and Italian musical traditions.

Italian Self Help

Many poorer Italians were able to start up businesses because they had the help of mutual aid societies. These were like private banks in which the immigrants pooled their money to provide each other with loans and insurance policies. The societies also helped to fund schools, medical clinics, pharmacies, restaurants, and even job-placement services. They were crucial in helping Italian immigrants establish themselves as respectable, well-educated members of South American society.

"Italianizing" South America

The Italians were not isolated in Italian-only suburbs or ghettos but integrated well into the culture of South America, and even influenced it. They found it relatively easy to pick up the new languages of Spanish and Portuguese, both of which have the same roots as Italian. Today the common spoken language of Buenos Aires is a unique blend of Argentine Spanish and Italian.

They also shared the Roman Catholic religion with the South Americans, and this enabled intermarriage between the two cultures, which helped the Italians to mix with local families and local culture.

Rural Brazil

Not all of the Italians who went to South America settled in the cities. Many became small farmers in rural Brazil.

The Brazilian government recruited many peasants by offering to pay their travel costs from Italy, to provide them with implements and seed, and to allow them to purchase their new farms gradually, with payments spread over ten years. It would be many years before any of these immigrants saw Italy again, so they were encouraged to come as families rather than as single men.

A Jungle Community

Between 1875 and 1914, 80,000 Italian peasants from northern Italy settled in the jungle of Rio Grande do Sol, a particularly isolated part of Brazil, and carved out small subsistence farms for themselves.

The journey was exhausting: a long steamship journey from Genoa to Brazil, followed by a riverboat journey inland, and eventually a long trek on foot or mule into the heart of the uninhabited jungle. The journey was bewildering, especially the trip through the jungle, with its snaking vines, towering trees, and terrifying animals such as jaguars, pythons, and monkeys. And finally, when they arrived, the newcomers found little to comfort them: just an area of uncleared land in the jungle and crude, temporary huts for shelter.

Building a Life

Most survived at first by selling wild fruits from the jungle, but eventually, after they had chopped down trees and cleared the vines, they created tiny but well-organized farms on which they grew corn, beans, wheat, and potatoes and raised pigs and chickens. Grapes were grown from vine cuttings the immigrants had brought with them from Italy.

▲ A settler's hut in southern Brazil. The early Italian farmers in the Brazilian jungle built simple one-roomed wooden huts, gradually adding on extra rooms as their farms prospered.

The settlements were extremely isolated, cut off from the rest of Brazilian society. Many of the immigrants suffered terrible homesickness. But gradually, little Italian townships grew up in the middle of the jungle, and in each one the immigrants built a tiny Roman Catholic chapel and joined together to pay for a priest from Italy to come and live in their midst. With the arrival of the priest, the immigrants could begin to feel that they were re-creating some of the habits and traditions of Italy that they had left behind.

The Shift to North America

Italian immigration to South America peaked in the early 1890s. After that, economic depression in the Brazilian coffee industry and a shortage of new farming land in Argentina and Brazil helped to make the United States the main destination of Italian emigrants. Between 1880 and 1920, roughly five million Italians went to the United States. Nearly all were looking for *pane e lavoro* – bread and work.

New Emigrants from the South

Unlike the immigration to Brazil and Argentina, southern Italians dominated immigration to the United States. In the 1890s, new factories in the north of Italy provided jobs for many northern Italians. The south, however, remained undeveloped. High taxes and a terrible agricultural depression in the 1890s finally tore many southern peasants away from their farms and villages.

Getting to the United States by steamship was cheap and easy. Settling into American life was, however, a different matter. Generally, the southern Italians knew less about the outside world than earlier emigrants from the north. Many were illiterate (could not read or write), and few had any business experience. To outsiders, their religious and social customs seemed old-fashioned. Because of these differences, the southerners were often seen as stupid and ignorant. They were also much darker than the fair-skinned northerners. Racists who wanted a whites-only immigration policy for the United States accused them of being too much like Africans. In addition, their loyalty to their family and village was sometimes criticized as being unpatriotic or "un-American."

Italians waiting to sail to America from the Italian port of Genoa. In 1900, it cost less to travel from Italy to New York than from Italy to Paris.

Chain Emigration

Reports of racism and anti-Italian feeling did not stop the immigrants from coming. With no money to invest in farmland, most of them headed for factory and construction work in the big industrial cities of the north, such as New York, Chicago, and Philadelphia. Some found railway and mining work in the western United States, while others worked in California's vineyards.

The dream of American wealth was strong. Sometimes a chain of emigration could shift almost the whole population of a village from Italy to the United States. The mayor of a small town in Italy used to greet visiting officials with: "I welcome you in the name of all six thousand inhabitants of this town. Three thousand are in America and the others are preparing to go."

A Slow Start to Success

For the Italians, finding financial success was much harder in the United States than in South America. They never dominated any city's working population as they had in Buenos Aires and so found themselves fighting for low-paying jobs with other unskilled laborers such as the Irish and the freed slaves. In New York many Italian men became barbers and shoe cleaners. The shops they started were small and often lacked the money and equipment to grow bigger. They made a profit mainly by relying upon the cheap labor of their families.

There were many reasons for this slow start. In addition to the common anti-Italian feeling and their own lack of skills, many of the immigrants had problems

▲ Italian arrivals in New York lining up at the Ellis Island reception center to prove that they are healthy and respectable enough to be allowed into the United States.

▼ Italians building roads in New York. Many Italian immigrants were able to find only low-paying manual work in the United States.

▲ Italian communities abroad still hold their religious festivals. Above, the Italian community in New York celebrates the feast of San Gennaro.

▼ Italians in North America often faced anti-Catholic prejudice. These Italian children in Canada were attending a missionary school that was trying to convert them to Protestantism.

learning English. There was also strong hostility to Catholics, and even the Irish, who dominated the Roman Catholic Church in the United States, thought that the Italians were too showy in their worship. They particularly did not like the Italians' colorful street festivals, in which they paraded images of the Madonna and saints covered with dollar bills. Until they were able to build their own churches, many Italian Catholics found themselves confined to worship in the basement of Irish churches.

Helping Each Other

To combat the difficulties of life in America, the immigrants lived closely together in tight-knit neighborhoods and formed their own protective institutions and organizations. As in South America, this included mutual-aid societies, but they never worked quite as well in the United States because the immigrants did not have enough money to build up big reserves of capital. The way the immigrants stuck together in their own local and regional groups also weakened the mutual-aid societies by keeping them small and divided.

One self-help society was the Scalabrini Fathers, who were a group of Italian Roman Catholic priests. They organized immigrants to build over a hundred schools and churches, mainly in New York, Chicago, and New England. They also set up a religious college, an old people's home, and an Italian-language newspaper. Such activities by this and other societies encouraged the immigrants to see that, against opposition, they were putting down solid roots in the United States.

The *Padrone* System

Another, more controversial form of protective institution was the immigrants' reliance on *padroni,* or labor bosses. A *padrone* made all the arrangements for young men who wanted to go to the United States: the emigration documents, the steamship passage, and, most important of all, the job at the other end. He received a commission from the steamship company and sometimes from the employer. The workers also paid their *padrone* — their fees were deducted from the workers' wages.

This system tied the immigrant workers to a particular *padrone*. The more workers the *padrone* controlled, the more power he had over employers, steamship companies, and workers' organizations or trade unions. Local U.S. and Canadian employers complained about foreigners having so much power, and some social reformers protested that the *padroni* cheated the immigrants.

▲ Women of Italian descent chat in Mulberry Street, the heart of New York's "Little Italy." There is still a strong Italian community in New York.

A Necessary Evil

The immigrants themselves did not see the system as all bad. For men who could not read, write, or speak English, the *padrone* was their link with North America. They were prepared to take on the dirty and dangerous jobs in construction, railways, and mining if they could save money to buy more land back home. They knew that their *padrone* was taking a cut of their wages, but he was providing a service they could not do without. And while the wages might have looked dreadful to a local individual, they looked good to an Italian. By living cheaply in an all-male dormitory, an Italian worker could save over half his wages to send home to his family.

▲ Workmen from Venice recruited by a *padrone* to work on the railways in British Columbia, Canada.

Criminal Stereotypes

Controversy over the *padrone* system was linked to the notion that all Italians were criminals and had links with the Mafia. The Mafia, from southern Italy, started as a form of self-help or protection system. In the 1920s the Mafia in the United States became involved in the illegal sale of alcohol. Later they expanded their activities into other criminal areas.

Most Italian immigrants had nothing to do with these illegal activities, but soon they discovered that they were all thought to be criminals. This stereotype has lasted for decades. In the 1980s, a successful publisher of Italian descent complained that: "If you make it in this country and you have an Italian name people just assume you're with the mob."

The growing Anti-Italian Storm

By 1920 the United States had a settled population of Italian-Americans. Many Italians had eventually established successful businesses and shops, though few had moved into the professions of law, health care, or education. Unlike in South America, most Italians married within their own community, and they continued to live in "Little Italies," inner-city ghettos with Italian shops, churches, schools, and even street names.

In spite of their long residence in the United States and their hard work, they were still troubled by anti-Italian hostility. Crude stereotypes in films and newspapers depicted all Italians as thuggish criminals who were more loyal to their families or the Mafia than to the United States. After the First World War, as the flow of Italians to the United States showed no sign of slackening, the prejudice and racism against Italians grew even stronger.

Marlon Brando plays a Mafia leader in the American film *The Godfather.*

The Rise of Fascism

In the 1920s, Fascism, a new force in Italian politics, took a very different view of emigration.

In the late 19th century, Italy's leaders did not try to stop the millions of Italians leaving the country. In 1901 the government established an Emigration Commission to try to protect emigrants from being cheated by labor recruiters, but it did little else. Indeed some politicians thought that emigration was a good thing; there would be fewer problems if the poor left the country and the money that the emigrants sent home to their families boosted the Italian economy.

▲ Benito Mussolini (1883-1945). Mussolini led the Italians into Fascism and, eventually, war.

Fascism: A New Force in Italian Politics

In the 1920s, Fascism, a new force in Italian politics, took a very different view of emigration. Fascism is a political system which forces people to devote all their efforts to improving and glorifying their country. It is a totalitarian system, that means that the government has total control over the people and forbids criticism of its activities.

Italy's problems had not all been solved by unification in 1861. It was still a poor country, not fully industrialized, and with divisions between the north and the south. This made it a difficult country to govern. To many Italians, Fascism seemed to hold out hope for a stronger, more unified country. By 1925, a Fascist government, led by Benito Mussolini, had taken office and was determined to tackle Italy's problems. Unfortunately for Italy, many of Mussolini's schemes were unworkable, and his claims about the Fascists' achievements were often empty boasts.

▼ Italian women give the Fascist salute. Many Italians supported Mussolini and his determination to make Italy into a strong nation.

▼ The Italian army invades Ethiopia in 1936. The Italians rejoiced at the success of the invasion, but the rest of the world criticized Italy for its aggression against a peaceful country.

Fascism, Emigration, and Africa

Mussolini wanted Italians to take pride in their country. Italians should be ashamed of emigrating, he said, because it showed the world that Italy could not afford to feed its own people. In 1927 the Fascists banned emigration, unless it was to one of Italy's African colonies.

For decades Italy had been trying to build an empire to rival the empires of Britain, France, Belgium, and Germany. In the 1880s Italy had established the colony of Italian Somaliland in East Africa. Libya was conquered in 1912, and in 1935 Mussolini ordered the invasion of Ethiopia. Maintaining the colonies cost a lot of money, and Mussolini encouraged Italians to settle there to make the colonies more profitable and to build up the glory of the Italian empire.

Italian laborers, farmers, and businessmen did go to Africa in large numbers, but often not to the Italian colonies. Seasonal laborers were more likely to go to vineyards in Tunisia or construction sites in Egypt (such as the Suez Canal). Some went farther away and set up farms in Nyasaland (modern Malawi) and South Africa.

The American Door Shuts

In truth, the Fascist ban on emigration had little effect. The real limit on Italian emigration came from the receiving countries. In 1917 the U.S. government had introduced literacy tests for immigrants, which stopped people who could not read and write from entering the country. This affected many of the poorly educated Italians from the south. In 1921 the government ruled that only 40,000 Italians per year would be allowed to enter the United States, and in 1924 this was cut back to only 4,000. The U.S. government had given in to the protests by

▲ Italian immigrants arrive in Libya. The Fascist government paid Italians to settle in Italy's African colonies.

▼ Italians in the United States celebrate Mussolini's invasion of Ethiopia.

labor organizations and racist groups. Shortly afterwards, Canada, Brazil, and Australia adopted similar policies. It did not matter what the Fascists had ordered; Italians were shut out of North America and Australia.

A worldwide Italian brotherhood

Mussolini's interest in emigration stretched beyond the Italians still at home. He called upon all Italians living overseas to defend Italy's place in the world. All over the world, Italians were encouraged to join local Fascist clubs, or *Fasci*. These were funded by the Italian government and were meant to encourage Italians abroad to promote the triumphs of Italian Fascism in their new countries.

Many Italians living abroad did indeed join *Fasci*. After years of being looked down upon as ignorant laborers, many were happy to celebrate Italy's achievements. It was the first time they could stand up and say to their host country: "I am proud to be an Italian." But very few of the Italians who joined these clubs were dedicated Fascists who supported a totalitarian style of government. They drank toasts to Mussolini, sang the Fascist anthem, and cheered the Fascist slogan: *Onore, Famiglia e Patria* (Honor, Family and Fatherland), but mostly they used the clubs as social clubs, as places to get together for Italian songs, food, and memories. Sadly, they could not foresee that soon, in the United States, Britain, France, Canada, and Australia, membership of a *Fasci* would be proof that they were enemies in their adopted countries.

Italians as Enemies Abroad

Men were taken away to camps and women and children left to fend for themselves.

In September 1939, Germany, led by the Fascist dictator Adolf Hitler, invaded Poland. In response, Britain and France declared war on Germany. The Second World War had begun. In June , 1940, Mussolini announced that Italy was joining the war on Germany's side. As a result, Italians who were living in the Allied countries were seen as enemies, especially those Italians who had joined the overseas Fascist clubs.

Shunned and Locked Up

The Allied countries included not only Britain and, after 1941, the United States, but also Australia, Canada, and South Africa. Throughout the Allied countries, Italian men were rounded up and interned in prisoner-of-war camps.

The rounding up of their menfolk was a disaster for Italian families. For five years, they were left without breadwinners. Women had to run shops and market gardens by themselves or beg for work from local employers. But in the anti-Italian atmosphere, no one wanted to buy goods from an Italian or employ one. Their businesses were vandalized, and children were picked on at school.

Italians Maria and Gino Paolini ran a small corner store in Sydney, Australia. After the war, Maria remembered:

Houses were searched, men taken away to camps for enemy aliens and women and children were left to fend for themselves. Gino was arrested and I was shunned by everybody — many customers stopped coming into the shop and vandals smashed the shop window.

Unable to keep the shop going, Maria took a job in a country poultry farm to keep herself and her son alive. She received no wages, only board and food. After the war, she and Gino had to rebuild their business from scratch.

▲ Once placed in an internment camp, like this one in the north of England, Italian-British men were unable to keep their jobs or support their families.

▼ This Italian chapel on the island of Orkney, Scotland, was built by Italian internees during the Second World War.

▲ Over 400 Italian-British internees died on the steamship *Arandora Star* when it was hit by a German torpedo off the coast of Ireland.

▼ Italy surrendered in September 1943, bringing relief to Italians living in Allied countries, such as this old lady from Mulberry Street in New York. She was born in Naples but eight of her American-born grandsons had joined the fight against Mussolini and Hitler.

The Tragedy of the *Arandora Star*

In Great Britain the war brought tragedy to the Italian community. On the night of June 10, 1940, anti-Italian riots broke out across Britain. Gangs vandalized, looted, and burned Italian cafés and shops in London, Liverpool, Cardiff, Belfast, Glasgow, and Edinburgh.

The next day the government rounded up hundreds of Italian men and boys and made arrangements to ship them to internment camps on the Isle of Wight or overseas. About 720 Italians were loaded onto the *Arandora Star* at Liverpool to sail to Canada, but on July 2, 1940, the ship was torpedoed by a German U-boat. It sank rapidly and over 700 men died, 446 of whom were Italians. For the rest of the war, their widows and children had to rely on the charity of the remaining hard-pressed Italians in Britain.

Starting All Over Again

In 1945 when Germany was defeated, the Italians in the Allied countries were set free. Many had bitter memories of their wasted years in the camps, and former businessmen often returned to find their shops empty. For most, the hard work of their early years as immigrants had to start all over again. They had to rebuild both their businesses and their friendships with the locals.

23

The Last Wave of Emigrants

Italy's economy was in such a bad state that the government calculated that another four or five million people would still have to emigrate.

▲ Bomb damage to the monastery of Monte Cassino. Toward the end of the war, the fighting in Italy between the Germans and the Allied forces destroyed many beautiful monuments.

Italy was devastated by the war: Bombing raids had destroyed towns, roads, factories, and farms. After 1945 the United States led an international effort to help Italy recover from the war damage, but Italy's economy was in such a bad state that the new Italian government calculated that another four or five million people would still have to emigrate.

The Italian people seemed to agree. Between 1946 and 1975, five million Italians emigrated to other neighboring European countries, mainly Austria, Germany, Switzerland, and France. Nine hundred thousand went to South America and half a million went to the United States, which in 1965 passed a law to select immigrants on the basis of their educational qualifications and work skills rather than their skin color and race. With this new law, the United States once again became a land of promise. Vito Calabrese, a professional violinist, immigrated to New York in 1965. As a boy in Venice during the war, he used to get tins of corned beef from American soldiers. He remembers his first impressions of the country:

My aunt had some relatives living in America. Right after the war they used to send us clothes. . . I remember that things were very hard. A very meager life. We liked to get those packages from America. That was my first impression of Americans — food from the soldiers and clothes from my aunt's relatives. The impression was of a country that had a lot of money.

In Britain, a special scheme between the Italian and British governments recruited several thousand young Italian women to work in factories in Lancashire, Cheshire, Yorkshire, and Derbyshire. Many of these women eventually settled in Britain and married either British men or immigrant workers from other war-torn countries, such as Poland.

▲ Plantations in Australia, such as this tea plantation in Queensland, provided work for many Italian immigrants.

Italian Immigration to Australia

Australia was another major destination for Italians after the war. The government wanted to increase the country's population to stop it from being taken over by an Asian country, so it advertised for immigrants from Europe.

Australia already had a small Italian population dating from the gold rushes in the 1850s. Pockets of Italian farmers and market gardeners existed around Mildura in Victoria and Griffith in New South Wales. Others worked as sugar cane cutters in Queensland or as gold miners in Kalgoorlie in Western Australia. After the war, this small population was joined by 270,000 new Italian immigrants, making them the largest non-English-speaking community in the country.

A Mixed Reception

The new immigrants had an unfriendly welcome. Initially many Australians shunned them and complained that the government was importing "blacks." To calm the population's fears about foreigners, the government promoted "assimilation." Assimilation meant that the immigrants should "mix in" and try to become like other Australians, speaking English instead of Italian and abandoning the customs and behaviors they had brought with them from Italy.

With local hostility running high, finding a job was not easy. In 1952, Italian men at the Bonegilla immigrant reception center in Victoria rioted because they were bored and frustrated at not being able to earn money. Eventually many found work in engineering and textile factories in Sydney, Melbourne, and Geelong and in the steelworks at Newcastle and Wollongong. Others worked on the Snowy Mountains Hydro-Electric Scheme, one of the country's biggest development projects, which was to generate electricity for many new postwar factories.

▲ Italian immigrants in Australia found work in factories and steelworks such as the Wollongong steelworks.

▲ Italian tailors and seamstresses recruited for the clothing industry in New York, Philadelphia, and Boston, arrive in the United States in 1956.

▼ Women working in a factory in Britain. For many Italian women, emigration brought with it the first chance to work outside the home and earn their own income.

Families and Homes

Two things were especially important to the immigrants: their families and homes. In 1969 the Australian government agreed to help Italian men bring their families to Australia. Gradually, the Italian population stopped being one of young men only. For some of the women, the shift to Australia gave them their first experience of having a paying job, perhaps as a factory hand, seamstress, or cleaner. The work was drudgery and low paying, but for some women it was a taste of freedom outside the home that they did not expect to get in Italy.

"Proxy Brides"

Sometimes a single man acquired a wife from Italy without having met her. He would ask his family to choose a bride for him, and she would then have a full wedding ceremony in Italy by herself, before sailing to Australia to meet her new husband. These brides were known as "proxy brides" because at their weddings their husbands were only present by proxy – not actually there but represented instead, perhaps, by a photograph. It could be a frightening experience for a young woman: sailing alone for weeks to an unknown country and then taken by a man she had never met to a small and isolated country town where no one but her new husband spoke Italian.

After family reunion, home ownership was the next goal for most immigrants. By 1980, 90 per cent of Italian families in Australia had bought or were buying their own homes. After a lifetime of poverty in Italy, the chance to own a home in Australia was too good to be missed.

Postwar Immigration to Canada

Canada was another country that saw its small Italian community grow into a large one after the Second World War. Over 400,000 Italians entered Canada between 1945 and 1975. Most came from Calabria, Abruzzi, Sicily, and Friuli, and most went to the province of Ontario, especially its capital city of Toronto. Today up to a quarter of Toronto's 2.5 million people can claim Italian descent.

Building Modern Canada

Most of the immigrants worked in the construction industry as unskilled laborers, even though many of them had skills as stonemasons, carpenters, tailors, or mechanics. Throughout the 1950s and 1960s, Italian sweat and muscle built the subway systems and tower blocks of Canada's modern cities, especially Toronto and Montreal. The work was often unsafe. In 1960 six Italian laborers were killed when a tunnel they were digging for a Toronto subway caved in. Accidents like this encouraged the immigrants to organize themselves into trade unions. Today, as in Argentina, the Italians are a strong force in Canadian labor organizations.

Out of the building boom, too, came a class of wealthy Italian housing developers and industrialists, plus thousands of suburban houses. Built by Italians, many were eventually bought by Italians as their first Canadian homes.

▼ The skyline of Montreal, Canada. Much of modern Montreal was built by Italian workers.

Italy's Economic Miracle

Wages rose and the national wealth soared.

In the 1970s, emigration from Italy suddenly stopped. The money invested after the war had finally worked its magic. Industries built by the postwar reconstruction program started to be profitable, wages rose, and the national wealth soared. Living standards, health care, and education all improved. More than a century after the shaky unification of 1861, Italy was able to support all of its people without sending them overseas.

Europe Looks at Italy Anew

Italy's prosperity and the sudden end of emigration helped to bring about a big change in European attitudes toward Italians. For decades Italians had been considered the poor migrant laborers of western Europe. Prosperity, however, made all the difference.

In 1957 Italy became a founding member of the Common Market (the European Economic Community, now the European Union), which helped to establish equality with France and Germany. Italian products, such as Vespa scooters, Zanussi refrigerators, and Benetton knitware, became household names all over Europe. Italy soon became famous for success in fashion, soccer, and design.

The Future for America's Italians

In the United States, too, the 12 million Italian-Americans began to throw off the old stereotype of Italians as ignorant, criminal laborers. Education played a big part in this improvement. Many of the early Italian immigrants taught their children that success was achieved not through education but by working hard in family businesses. Racism had taught them to believe that they or their children would never be accepted in the United States as professionals like teachers, doctors, and lawyers.

◀ **Roberto Baggio, one of Italy's world-class soccer players. Today, Italy is one of the dominant soccer-playing nations.**

By 1945, the emphasis on hard work, family loyalty, and business meant that while many Italian-Americans had become wealthy, they were not well represented in jobs that required a college education. The dislike and mistrust of higher education began to disappear in the 1970s. Italian-Americans now frequently qualify as lawyers, social workers, and college teachers.

As the immigrants and their children and grandchildren have become wealthier and more middle-class, the old Italian inner-city communities have begun to break up, and some of the old mutual-aid societies, charitable orders, and religious festivals have disappeared. But even as this happens, young Italian-Americans are enrolling in Italian classes to learn about the language and culture of their grandparents.

More Arrivals than Departures

Italians have long been used to former emigrants returning home. In the early 20th century, returnees (or *rimpatriati*) had a big impact on the Italian economy and also its culture, bringing back with them new ideas and fashions that they had acquired abroad. Italians were surprised, however, to discover that the postwar economic success completely reversed the old migration pattern.

In the 1970s and 1980s, thousands of people from Africa, the Philippines, and eastern Europe arrived in Italy, usually as tourists, and attempted to stay on as permanent citizens. Italy was unprepared for the flood of immigrants. Many Italians complained about the arrival of black people and accused them of taking jobs from locals, of reducing wages, and of making the streets dirty and unsafe. Gradually the Italian government has created laws to regulate the arrival of new immigrants and protect those already settled in Italy. Like the people in the countries that received Italian immigrants, Italians are now learning how to accept and appreciate people from different cultures in their society.

▼ This luxurious shopping arcade in the city of Milan is proof of Italy's postwar prosperity.

▼ Refugees from Albania flooded into Italy in the early 1990s after the collapse of the Albanian economy. After over 100 years of immigrating to other countries, Italians now found that outsiders wanted to share in their country's new wealth.

Timeline

c.200 BC–AD 500   Roman Empire: At the height of the empire, the emperor in Rome ruled over most of southern and central Europe, the Middle East, North Africa, France, England, and Wales.

c.1300–1600   The Renaissance: Italy leads western Europe in art, literature, philosophy, architecture, commerce, and manufacturing; the Renaissance artists look back to and strive to copy the achievements of the Roman Empire.

1492   Charles VIII of France conquers Naples. This is the beginning of almost 400 years of French, Spanish, and Austrian invasion and conquest of different Italian states.

1760s   A series of disastrous famines hits Italy and thousands of peasants starve to death. The famines show the need for government reform and economic and agricultural improvement.

c.1800–1870   The period of the *Risorgimento*: the movement for Italian unity and opposition to French and Austrian intervention in Italian politics.

1850s   Migration by craft workers and musicians means that distinct Italian suburbs exist in many European cities, as well as in New York in the United States and Buenos Aires in Argentina.

1860–61   Giuseppe Garibaldi defeats the rulers of southern Italy; Victor Emmanuel II, king of Piedmont-Sardinia in the north, becomes the first king of a united Italy.

1864   St. Peter's, the first Italian church in Britain, is founded in Clerkenwell, London; in 1883 a street procession of the Madonna del Carmine starts from the church; this procession is still held every year on the first Sunday after July 6.

1866   St. Anthony's, the first Italian church in America, is founded in New York.

1883   Europe's first central electricity-generating plant opens in Milan, a hydroelectric scheme powered by Italy's alpine rivers. The electricity powers an industrial boom in northern Italy with new factories and bigger, wealthier cities; meanwhile the south stays poor.

1890s   Severe agricultural depression in southern Italy forces many southern peasants to migrate.

1891   Eleven Italian immigrants are lynched (killed by a mob of people) in New Orleans; other lynchings in Louisiana occur in 1896 and 1899.

1893   Nine Italian workers are murdered and hundreds assaulted at Aigues Mortes, southern France.

1914–18   First World War. In May 1915, Italy becomes an ally of Britain against Germany and the Austro-Hungarian Empire. Many Italian men living abroad return home to fight for Italy. At the end of the war, Italy faces economic and administrative weaknesses that pave the way for the rise of Fascism.

1917   The U.S. begins to limit Italian immigration; strict quotas on Italian arrivals are applied in 1921.

1921   The Fascists form a national party, Partito Nazionale Fascista, with Benito Mussolini as its leader. Squads of violent young men take advantage of the lack of law and order to attack trade union leaders and social reformers.

1924   The United States put large restrictions on Italian immigration; soon Australia, Canada, and Brazil adopt similar anti-Italian policies.

1925   Opposition to Mussolini's leadership evaporates,and he leads Italy with a totalitarian Fascist government.

1927   The Fascists ban emigration of working men, except to Italy's African colonies.

1935–36   Italy invades and conquers Ethiopia; many other countries condemn Italian aggression.

1939–45   Second World War: Italy sides with Hitler's Germany to fight against Britain and its allies. In Britain and Allied countries, Italian men are sent to internment camps as enemy aliens. Italy itself suffers severe war damage and the loss of its African colonies. In April 1945, Allied forces and Italian resistance fighters finally defeat Fascism in Italy; Mussolini is executed.

1946   Italy becomes a republic and begins to rebuild its economy and administration.

1957   Italy, along with France and Germany, is a founding member of the Common Market (European Economic Community, now the European Union).

1965   The United States stops using people's race to determine whether they can be immigrants or not. Italians willing to do laboring jobs are again accepted in the United States. Canada (and in 1973 Australia too) also stops racist immigration laws.

1965–75   Italy's "Economic Miracle" takes effect and emigration from Italy dries up.

June 1970   Italian-Americans hold mass demonstrations in New York to protest against the stereotyping of them as criminals and Mafiosi (members of the Mafia).

1982   Italy's soccer team wins the World Cup. All over the world, Italians and people of Italian descent join in the celebrations.

Glossary

ally: A friend or supporter. In war, allies are countries that fight together against an enemy country.

bauxite: A rock that is the main source of the metal aluminum.

breadwinner: The person in a family who earns the money that buys the food and pays for the family's housing, or the person in a family with the biggest wage.

capital: In a shop or business, the money that is reserved for buying new equipment or buildings. A shop that does not have a good reserve of capital cannot grow bigger or more successful.

colony: A country or territory that has been taken over by another country and is ruled by that country.

commerce: The buying and selling of things, usually on a big scale.

deforestation: The clearing or removal of trees from land.

dialect: The language of a particular region or district that differs in certain words and sometimes grammar from the standard language of the whole country.

emigrate: To leave one's country to settle permanently in another country.

empire: A group of nations or countries ruled over by one single powerful country.

ghetto: An area or suburb of a city in which a minority population lives.

illiterate: Not able to read or write.

immigrate: To arrive in a foreign country intending to stay there permanently.

industrialist: A person who puts money and ideas into creating big industrial companies, such as mines, factories, or transport businesses.

industrialization: The shift from making individual things by hand to mass-producing them cheaply with machines.

internee: Someone who has been interned, or imprisoned.

literacy: The ability to read and write.

Madonna: The Virgin Mary, the mother of Jesus Christ.

market garden: A small farm, often run by a single family, that produces vegetables and sometimes fruit and flowers for sale in markets. Often the gardening work is done by hand rather than by machines.

organ-grinder: The person who operates a barrel or hand organ by turning its handle.

padrone/(plural padroni): The Italian word for patron. For poor Italian emigrants, a *padrone* was someone who found them work abroad and arranged their transport, accommodation, and wages. Often he took a large chunk of their wages to pay for his services, so that it was hard for some workers ever to earn enough money to become independent of him. A *padrone* had a lot of power over the poor workers who accepted his help.

patriot: Someone who loves his or her country and will fight to defend it against outsiders.

peninsula: A strip of land, often a long and narrow one, that projects into the sea.

policy: A plan or set of laws and regulations created to achieve a goal. Governments make policies which they hope will achieve the best for the people of their country.

prejudice: An opinion against someone or something that has been made irrationally — without knowing anything about that person or subject.

prosperity: Wealth. A country with a good economy and most of its people in employment is a prosperous one.

Protestantism: A form of Christianity that does not accept that the Pope is God's leader on Earth and that rejects some of the practices and beliefs of the Roman Catholic Church. Protestants believe that they have a direct relationship with God and do not accept that the Pope or the Virgin Mary or saints can speak to God on their behalf.

racism: Judging people by their race or by the color of their skin.

Roman Catholic: A Christian who recognizes the Pope as God's representative on Earth and who accepts his interpretation of the Bible.

seasonal workers: Workers who earn their wages by getting jobs that only happen at particular times of the year, such as harvest work in the summer or hotel work during busy tourist periods.

subsistence: The state of earning just enough to live on; a subsistence farm is one that produces just enough to keep the farmer's family alive.

trade union: An organization or club of workers who work in the same type of employment and support each other in getting better wages and conditions from their employers. For example, all the workers on a city's building sites may belong to a single building-workers' trade union.

unify: To bring or join together.

Index